W9-AIA-146

COMMUNITY · CONNECTIONS

?

GETTING TO KNOW OUR PLANET
CANADIAN TAIGA

BY VICKY FRANCHINO

Published in the United States of America by Cherry Lake Publishing
Ann Arbor, Michigan
www.cherrylakepublishing.com

Content Adviser: Linda M. Hooper-Bùi, PhD, Associate Professor,
Department of Environmental Science, Louisiana State University
Agricultural Center, Baton Rouge, Louisiana
Reading Adviser: Marla Conn, Read With Me Now

Photo Credits: Cover and pages 1, 7, and 9, © Pi-Lens/Shutterstock.com; page 5, © Serjio74/
Shutterstock.com; page 11, © Matthew Jacques/Shutterstock.com; page 13, © Agustin Esmoris/
Shutterstock.com; page 15, © Tom Reichner/Shutterstock.com; page 17, © Kokhanchikov/
Shutterstock.com; page 19, © Hemis/Alamy Stock Photo; page 21, © Bluegreen Pictures/
Alamy Stock Photo.

LIBRARY OF CONGRESS CATALOGING-IN-PUBLICATION DATA
Names: Franchino, Vicky, author.
   Title: Canadian taiga / by Vicky Franchino.
Other titles: Community connections (Cherry Lake Publishing)
Description: Ann Arbor, Michigan : Cherry Lake Publishing, [2016] | 2014" |
   Series: Community connections | Series: Getting to know our planet |
   Audience: K to grade 3. | Includes bibliographical references and index.
Identifiers: LCCN 2015032304| ISBN 9781634705158 (lib. bdg.) |
   ISBN 9781634706353 (pbk.) | ISBN 9781634705752 (pdf) |
   ISBN 9781634706957 (ebook)
Subjects: LCSH: Taigas—Canada—Juvenile literature. | Taiga ecology—Canada—Juvenile
   literature. | Forests and forestry—Canada—Juvenile literature.
Classification: LCC QK938.T34 F73 2016 | DDC 577.3/70971—dc23 LC record
available at http://lccn.loc.gov/2015032304

Cherry Lake Publishing would like to acknowledge the
work of The Partnership for 21st Century Skills. Please
visit www.p21.org for more information.

Printed in the United States of America
Corporate Graphics
January 2016

CONTENTS

GETTING TO KNOW OUR PLANET

A COLD, GREEN WORLD

The Canadian **taiga** is cold and green most of the year. On a winter day, the temperature can drop as low as –40 degrees Fahrenheit (–40 degrees Celsius). Winter days are short. In summer, the days are long and sunny. The temperature might climb as high as 70°F (21°C). Summer doesn't last long, though!

Green taiga covers a huge portion of Canada.

ASK QUESTIONS!

Taiga is a Russian word that means "marshy pine forest." It is pronounced TYE-ga. What questions do you have about the taiga? Before you start to read, write them down. See if the answers are in this book!

5

The taiga is filled with **conifers**. These are trees with cones and needles. Unlike other trees, conifers don't lose their leaves in winter. They stay green all year long. This is what gives the taiga its unique appearance.

Conifers stay green even during the heavy snow of winter.

Not many different kinds of trees can grow in the taiga. Why do you think this is? Think about the weather in the taiga.

7

A SOGGY LAND

The Canadian taiga is very wet. However, only 8 to 40 inches (20 to 101.6 centimeters) of rain and snow fall there each year. Then why is it so soggy? One reason is because it isn't very sunny most of the time. Moisture doesn't **evaporate** quickly without sunlight.

Ponds and marshy areas are common throughout the taiga.

LOOK!

Does water evaporate quickly where you live? The next time it rains, watch how long it takes for wet sidewalks and puddles to dry up.

9

Much of the ground in the taiga is frozen solid. This hard soil can't absorb water. In some parts of the taiga, there is also a layer of rock called the Canadian Shield. This stops the soil beneath from soaking up water.

Lichen and moss can grow on even the rockiest ground.

MAKE A GUESS!

Lichen, moss, and fungi all grow well in the taiga. The roots of these plants do not reach deep underground. Why do you think this is important in the taiga?

11

CREATURES OF THE NORTH

Many animals live in the taiga. These animals all have ways of dealing with the extreme cold of winter. Animals such as caribou and moose have fur that keeps them warm. Bears, chipmunks, and snakes **hibernate** when the temperature drops. Squirrels hide food before the first snow. They dig it up later when they get hungry.

Grizzly bears are among the many animal species of the Canadian taiga.

MAKE A GUESS!

The snowshoe hare has brown fur in the summer and white fur in the winter. Why do you think this is helpful? Keep in mind that many animals hunt hares for food.

13

Birds such as hawks, eagles, and sparrows fly to warmer areas when temperatures begin to drop. They return to the taiga in spring. Other birds stay in the taiga all winter. Chickadees lower their body temperature to stay alive when it is very cold. Grouse make protective nests out of snow. Many birds build cozy homes inside hollow trees.

Grouse are right at home in snowy weather.

THINK!

The taiga's trees are slowly disappearing. People cut them down to make paper and other things out of the wood. Think about ways you could use fewer paper products. Using less paper helps preserve trees!

15

The taiga buzzes with insects during summer. Mosquitoes and biting black flies are everywhere. These insects can make it unpleasant to be outside. Some insects travel to the taiga as the days grow longer and warmer. Others lay eggs in the fall. These eggs hatch in spring.

Mosquitoes leave behind itchy, red bumps when they bite.

LOOK!

What kinds of insects do you notice in your backyard? Are there mosquitoes and biting flies where you live? What do you do to protect yourself from them?

17

PEOPLE OF THE TAIGA

Many people live in the taiga. The Cree are **native** people who have made the taiga their home for hundreds of years. Long ago, they lived off the land. They hunted and fished for food. They used plants for medicine and trees for shelter. More than half of Canada's native people live in the taiga.

A Cree man traps a mink in the taiga.

Can you imagine
living in the taiga?
How would you spend
your time in the long
days of summer?
What would you do
for fun during the
dark, cold winter?

19

Life in the taiga can be difficult. It is hard to travel from one place to another. This makes it tough to get food and other supplies. Also, the cold weather can be very unpleasant. However, the taiga is a beautiful, green land. Would you like to live there?

If you want to live in remote wilderness, the taiga might be the place for you.

Use what you've learned about the Canadian taiga to create a piece of art. You could draw a picture of the taiga. Or you could build a model of the taiga using clay and other art supplies. The choice is up to you!

21

GLOSSARY

conifers (KAH-nuf-furz) evergreen trees that produce their seeds in cones

evaporate (i-VAP-uh-rate) to change from a liquid to a vapor or gas

hibernate (HY-bur-nate) to sleep through the winter in order to survive when temperatures are cold and food is hard to find

native (NAY-tiv) a person who was born in or lives in a particular place

taiga (TYE-ga) the forested area just south of the tundra

FIND OUT MORE

BOOKS

Day, Trevor. *Taiga*. Chicago: Raintree, 2010.

Johansson, Philip. *The Taiga: Discover This Forested Biome*. Berkeley Heights, NJ: Enslow Elementary, 2015.

WEB SITES

National Geographic: Taiga
http://education.nationalgeographic.com/encyclopedia/taiga/
Learn more about the plants and animals that make the taiga home.

World Wildlife Fund: Canadian Boreal Forests
*http://wwf.panda.org/about_our_earth/ecoregions
/canadian_boreal_forests.cfm*
Find out more about life in the Canadian taiga.

INDEX

ABOUT THE AUTHOR

Vicky Franchino likes to learn new things about the places, animals, and plants that can be found in different areas around the world. One interesting thing that she learned while writing this book: The shape of conifer trees makes it easy for snow to slide right off them! Vicky lives in Wisconsin with her family and will spend this winter wishing her hometown got only as much snow as the taiga!